The Forest in the Trees

by Connie McLennan

Deep in the woods
near a foggy sea,
there's a hidden forest
in the trees.

Coast redwoods only grow in a narrow band of land near the Pacific Ocean in northern California and southern Oregon.

Even though the oldest redwoods have lived over 2,500 years, it was not until the late 1990s that scientists discovered how many plants and animals live high in their branches, hundreds of feet above the ground.

These are the trunks,
massive and tall,
that lead to the forest
in the trees.

Coast redwoods are the world's tallest trees. The tallest redwood known measures nearly 379 feet (115 m) — as tall as a 37-story building!

After shade from the upper branches causes lower branches to die, redwood trunks can rise more than 250 feet (76 m) before the first big limbs appear — 25 stories up. This makes climbing them dangerous and difficult. To study the hidden forest above, scientists called botanists use ropes to climb high into the trees.

These are the sprouts,
new little trees;
shooting from trunks,
massive and tall;
that lead to the forest
in the trees.

When the top of a redwood dies or breaks off in a storm, new trunks may sprout up from large limbs, or out from the trunk, and grow upward like the main tree. All these new trees growing from the old tree are called reiterations. One of the biggest redwoods contains 220 trunk reiterations!

This is the soil,
   humid and deep;
collecting by sprouts,
   new little trees;
shooting from trunks,
   massive and tall;
that lead to the forest
   in the trees.

The world at the top of the forest is called the canopy.

Fallen redwood leaves and twigs collect on limbs and in notches between trunks. Over time this debris breaks down to form sponge-like mats called humus. In places, layers of this organic canopy soil can be several feet (up to a meter) deep.

These are the bugs,
    crawling or leaping;
enriching the soil,
    humid and deepening;
collecting by sprouts,
    new little trees;
shooting from trunks,
    massive and tall;
that lead to the forest
    in the trees.

Mites, beetles, worms, and other bugs live in the canopy soil, eating the decomposing leaves and wood. Tiny springtails have tail-like limbs folded beneath their bodies they use to jump when they are threatened.

Sow bugs and pill bugs actually are not bugs. They are crustaceans, like shrimp, that breathe through gills just like their marine relatives. They are the only crustaceans that live on land.

This is the creature,
  slender and blotchy;
munching on bugs,
  crawling or leaping;
enriching the soil,
  humid and deepening;
collecting by sprouts,
  new little trees;

shooting from trunks,
  massive and tall;
that lead to the forest
  in the trees.

Wandering salamanders breathe through their skin and mouths instead of lungs.

Some live their entire lives in the moist redwoods, eating tiny bugs they find in the humus.

Most are brown with gold, greenish, or reddish blotches that work as camouflage in the wood and leaves.

These are the ferns,
  soggy and heavy;
hiding the creature,
  slender and blotchy;
munching on bugs,
  crawling or leaping;
enriching the soil,
  humid and deepening;
collecting by sprouts,
  new little trees;
shooting from trunks,
  massive and tall;
that lead to the forest
  in the trees.

Plants that grow on other plants are called epiphytes. Hundreds of epiphytes live in the redwood canopy.

Huge masses of hanging ferns growing in canopy humus are called fern mats. When soaked with rain, they can weigh as much as a car and are heavier than the epiphytes in any of the tropical rain forest canopies.

This is the bush,
  bursting with berries;
blooming near ferns,
  soggy and heavy;
hiding the creature,
  slender and blotchy;
munching on bugs,
  crawling or leaping;
enriching the soil,
  humid and deepening;
collecting by sprouts,
  new little trees;
shooting from trunks,
  massive and tall;
that lead to the forest
  in the trees.

Several types of shrubs including huckleberry, elderberry, salmonberry, gooseberry, and currant grow everywhere in the redwood canopy.

Some bushes produce fruit that botanists can eat as they climb and study the trees.

This is the lichen,
  lacy and airy;
up by the bush,
  bursting with berries;
blooming near ferns,
  soggy and heavy;
hiding the creature,
  slender and blotchy;
munching on bugs,
  crawling or leaping;

enriching the soil,
  humid and deepening;
collecting by sprouts,
  new little trees;
shooting from trunks,
  massive and tall;
that lead to the forest
  in the trees.

A wide variety of lichens in wild shapes and colors grow all over the redwood canopies. Lichens are actually two organisms growing together. The lace lichen is an official state symbol of California.

Because lichens are sensitive to air pollution and climate, scientists are using them to monitor air quality and climate change.

This is the squirrel,
  tiny and quiet;
sailing past lichen,
  lacy and airy;
up by the bush,
  bursting with berries;
blooming near ferns,
  soggy and heavy;
hiding the creature,
  slender and blotchy;
munching on bugs,
  crawling or leaping;

enriching the soil,
  humid and deepening;
collecting by sprouts,
  new little trees;
shooting from trunks,
  massive and tall;
that lead to the forest
  in the trees.

Humboldt flying squirrels don't really fly. They jump from the trees and sail like gliders as far as 150 feet (46 m) using membranes stretched between their arms and legs. Then they use their fluffy tails to steer and slow down before landing in the next tree.

Unlike other squirrels, flying squirrels come out mostly at night, cruising from tree to tree in search of food. During the day they sleep in tree holes lined with soft moss or lichens.

This is the owl,
  spotty and silent;
hunting the squirrel,
  tiny and quiet;
sailing past lichen,
  lacy and airy;
up by the bush,
  bursting with berries;
blooming near ferns,
  soggy and heavy;
hiding the creature,
  slender and blotchy;
munching on bugs,
  crawling or leaping;
enriching the soil,
  humid and deepening;
collecting by sprouts,
  new little trees;
shooting from trunks,
  massive and tall;
that lead to the forest
  in the trees.

Northern spotted owls watch from a perch, then swoop out to catch flying squirrels, small rodents, birds, or reptiles. They flap their wings quickly to gain speed, then glide silently down to catch the prey in their talons.

Instead of building their own nests, spotted owls nest in tree cavities, broken treetops, and the old nests of hawks, eagles, and squirrels.

This is the laurel,
   leafy and fragrant;
above with the owl,
   spotty and silent;
hunting the squirrel,
   tiny and quiet;
sailing past lichen,
   lacy and airy;
up by the bush,
   bursting with berries;
blooming near ferns,
   soggy and heavy;
hiding the creature,
   slender and blotchy;
munching on bugs,
   crawling or leaping;
enriching the soil,
   humid and deepening;

collecting by sprouts,
   new little trees;
shooting from trunks,
   massive and tall;
that lead to the forest
   in the trees.

Most trees growing in the canopy are small. However, scientists have found both a 40-foot tall (12 m) hemlock and an eight-foot (2 m) spruce on the limbs of redwoods, hundreds of feet off the ground. They have also found bay laurel trees, fir trees, and tanoaks growing in the canopy.

This is the auk,
   plump and mysterious;
nesting near laurel,
   leafy and fragrant;
above with the owl,
   spotty and silent;
hunting the squirrel,
   tiny and quiet;
sailing past lichen,
   lacy and airy;
up by the bush,
   bursting with berries;
blooming near ferns,
   soggy and heavy;
hiding the creature,
   slender and blotchy;

munching on bugs,
   crawling or leaping;
enriching the soil,
   humid and deepening;
collecting by sprouts,
   new little trees;
shooting from trunks,
   massive and tall;
that lead to the forest
   in the trees.

Auks are diving seabirds that "fly" in the ocean as well as through the air. Marbled murrelets, a type of auk, eat mostly fish but build their nests high in the redwoods, several miles from shore. Their nests are only shallow dips in the moss and lichen on wide branches, where they hunker down to warm a single egg.

A murrelet sometimes flies as far as 50 miles (80 km) inland to nest and brings fish to its chick several times a day for a month. On its first flight, the fledgling chick then must fly all the way to the ocean!

For Creative Minds

Coast Redwood Habitat: Living or Nonliving?

Coast redwoods are native to a small area along the Pacific coast of northern California and southern Oregon. In all habitats and ecosystems, living things rely on both living things and nonliving things to survive. Can you identify which things found in the coast redwood habitat are living and which are nonliving?

Animals: From tiny insects to large black bears, a wide variety of animals live in and around the coast redwoods.

Water: This area has a moist climate that receives over 100 inches (2.5 m) of rain a year, plus fog from the ocean.

Temperature: Some plants grow in hot temperatures close to the equator (tropical), and others grow in cold temperatures far from the equator (polar). Between tropical and polar, temperatures are more temperate. The coast redwoods grow in a temperate climate.

Plants: Douglas firs, hemlocks, ferns, sorrels, mosses, and rhododendron can all be found in the understory of a healthy coast redwood habitat. Ferns, bushes, redwood sprouts, and even other kinds of trees can be found in the canopy.

Soil: Decaying plants, including coast redwoods, provide nutrients to the soil that are then used by other plants.

Answers: Living: animals, plants; Nonliving: water, temperature, soil

Redwood Forest Vocabulary Matching

Match the vocabulary description to the image.

1. Trunks that grow from limbs growing from the main trunk are called **reiterations**.

2. The world at the top of the forest is called a **canopy**.

3. Sponge-like mats of soil are called **humus**.

4. Plants called **epiphytes** attach themselves to other plants to grow.

5. Over 150 different types of **lichens** grow in the redwood canopies. Lichens are actually two organisms growing together.

6. Scientists who climb and study trees are called **botanists**.

Answers: 1-F, 2-D, 3-B, 4-A, 5-E, 6-C

Animals and Their Basic Needs

Many types of animals make their homes high in the canopy, the secret forest of the coast redwoods. Match the animal adaptations to how they provide their basic needs:

- How they **protect themselves** from becoming food for other animals.
- How they find or get **food and water**.
- How they get **oxygen (air)** from their surroundings.
- Where they live and raise young (**shelter**).

Pill bugs often roll themselves into balls when disturbed. Because of that, they are sometimes called roly-polies.

They breathe through gills.

Wandering salamanders breathe through their skin and mouths instead of lungs.

They eat tiny bugs crawling in the humus and camouflage themselves in the leaves to hide from predators.

During the day, Humboldt flying squirrels sleep in tree holes lined with soft moss or lichens.

They glide from tree to tree at night searching for food.

Northern spotted owls catch prey in their talons.

They nest in tree cavities, broken treetops, and in the old nests of hawks, eagles, and squirrels.

Marbled murrelets nest in shallow dips in moss and lichen high in the redwoods, far from their ocean home.

Parents will carry fish from the ocean to their young several times a day.

Answers: protect themselves: wandering salamanders, pill bugs/roly-polies; food & water: wandering salamanders, Humboldt flying squirrels, northern spotted owls, marbled murrelets; get oxygen (air): pill bugs/roly-polies, wandering salamanders; shelter: Humboldt flying squirrels, northern spotted owls, marbled murrelets

Making New Trees

All living things make new living things (reproduce). Match the coast redwood reproduction description to the correct image.

1. A mature coast redwood makes up to 100,000 small **cones** in a year. Each cone is about an inch long (2.5 cm) and has 50 to 100 tiny seeds (about the size of tomato seeds). Few of its seeds ever grow into new trees because the dense forest is too dark and crowded.

2. Most coast redwoods reproduce by **stump sprouts** growing out of large outgrowths on the tree trunk called **burls**. When a coast redwood tree is stressed by fire, drought, wind or human activity, the burl sends out shoots that are copies of the parent tree!

3. If these burls grow all around the tree, and the parent tree dies, the remaining circle of trees is called a **fairy ring**.

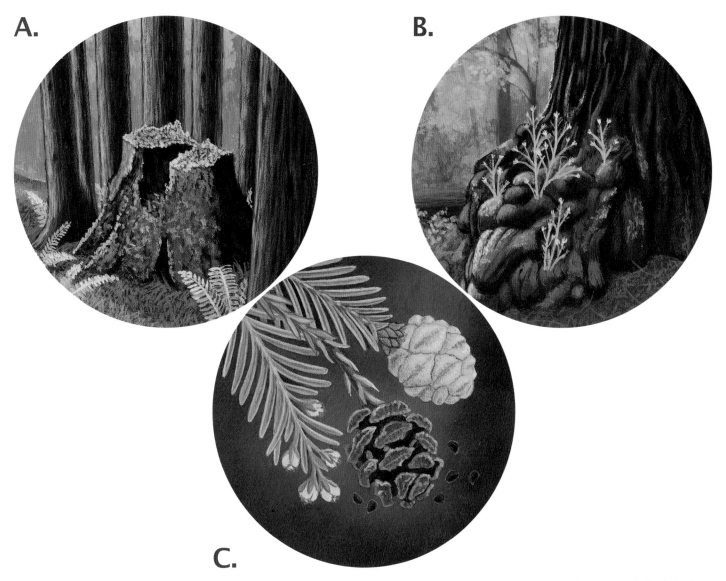

A.

B.

C.

Answers: 1-C, 2-B, 3-A

For my family with love and gratitude: my son Thomas, who read drafts and encouraged me to focus more quickly on the canopy, and husband Geoffrey, my "patron of the arts." Thanks to Richard Preston, whose 2005 New Yorker article "Climbing the Redwoods" first inspired this book, and to Donna & Lee German at Arbordale Publishing for their support.—CM

Thanks to Deborah Zierten, Education & Interpretation Manager for Save the Redwoods League for ensuring the accuracy of the information in this book.

Library of Congress Cataloging-in-Publication Data

Names: McLennan, Connie, author.
Title: The forest in the trees / by Connie McLennan.
Description: Mt. Pleasant, SC : Arbordale Publishing, [2019] | Audience: Age
    3-7. | Audience: K to Grade 3. | Includes bibliographical references.
Identifiers: LCCN 2018050176 (print) | LCCN 2018050549 (ebook) | ISBN
    9781643513539 (Pdf) | ISBN 9781643513553 (ePub3) | ISBN 9781643513577 (
    Read aloud interactive) | ISBN 9781643513508 (hardcover) | ISBN
    9781643513515 (paperback) |
Subjects: LCSH: Coast redwood--Ecology--California--Pacific Coast--Juvenile
    literature. | Coast redwood--Ecology--Oregon--Pacific Coast--Juvenile
    literature. | Forest canopy ecology--Juvenile literature.
Classification: LCC SD397.R3 (ebook) | LCC SD397.R3 M35 2019 (print) | DDC
    577.309794--dc23
LC record available at https://lccn.loc.gov/2018050176

Lexile® Level: 1070   key phrases: habitats, coast redwood, plant and animal interaction

Bibliography/ Bibliografía:
"About the Trees." Redwood National and State Parks California, February 28 2015. Internet. Accessed September 2018.
"Big Trees: A Bank for Soil Bugs." Save the Redwoods League, 28 July 2002. Internet. Accessed August 2018.
Boxall, Bettina. "Climate change may be speeding coast redwood, giant sequoia growth." Los Angeles Times, 14 August 2013.
Broughton, Eve. "Natural Life of the Lost Coast; the rollie-pollie." Redwood Times, 18 October 2013.
"California's State Lichen: Lace lichen (Ramalina menziesii)." The Lichen Society. Internet. Accessed August 2018.
Earle, Christopher J. "Sequoia sempervirens." The Gymnosperm Database 2017. Internet. Accessed August 2018.
Hadley, Debbie. "15 Fascinating Facts About Pill Bugs." Thought Company, 18 June, 2018. Internet. Accessed August 2018
Katz, Richard. "Plant Profile: The Redwood Tree." Flower Essence Society. Internet. Accessed August 2018.
"Marbled Murrelet." Audubon. Internet. Accessed August 2018.
Morell, Virginia. "Meet This Newly Discovered Flying Squirrel." National Geographic, 30 May 2017. Internet. Accessed August 2018.
"Northern Spotted Owls." National Park Service. Internet. Accessed August 2018.
Piper, Ross. Extraordinary animals: an encyclopedia of curious and unusual animals. Greenwood Press, 2007.
Preston, Richard1. "Climbing the Redwoods. The New Yorker, 14 & 15 February 2005,
Preston, Richard2. The Wild Trees: A Story of Passion and Daring. Random House (2007).
"Redwood Ed: A Guide to the Coast Redwoods for Teachers and Learners." California Department of Parks and Recreation,
    Internet. Accessed August 2018.
"Redwood Forest Facts: Trees in the Redwood Canopy." Save the Redwoods League. Internet. Accessed August 2018.
Sillett, Stephen C., James C. Spickler, and Robert Van Pelt. "Crown Structure of the World's Second Largest Tree." Madroño
    (2000): pp. 125-133. Internet. Accessed August 2018.
"Spotted Owl Life History." The Cornell Lab of Ornithology. Internet. Accessed August 2018
Skenhe, Jennifer. "Redwood Regeneration." Quest, 28 Feb. 2011. Internet. Accessed August 2018.
"Sponge-like Mats Make Good Habitat in Redwood Canopies: Wandering Salamanders Benefit." Save the Redwoods League, July
    28, 2000. Internet. Accessed August 2018.
Vaden, Mario. "Del Norte Titan Coast Redwood." M. D. Vaden. 2009-20017. Internet. Accessed August 2018.
Wake and Jackman. "Wandering Salamander - Aneides vagrans." CaliforniaHerps.com, 1999. Internet. Accessed August 2018.
"What is Growing in the Canopies of the Tallest Trees in the World?" Save the Redwoods League, 13 January 2017. Internet.
    Accessed August 2018.
Wheeler, Tom. "Meet Humboldt's Flying Squirrel, a New Species in our Forests." Environmental Protection Information Center,
    20 July 2017. Internet. Accessed August 2018.
Zierten, Deborah. " Introducing Our New State Lichen!" Save the Redwoods League. 14 August 2015. Internet. Accessed August 2018.

Printed in China, May 2019
This product conforms to CPSIA 2008
First Printing

Arbordale Publishing
Mt. Pleasant, SC 29464
www.ArbordalePublishing.com